# 25 Ways to Cook a Mouse

## for the Gourmet Cat

# 25 WAYS TO COOK A MOUSE

## *for the Gourmet Cat*

*Written & Illustrated by* ORSON BEAN

*Watercolored by* SUSANNAH BEAN

*A Birch Lane Press Book*
*Published by Carol Publishing Group*

A Birch Lane Press Book
Published by Carol Publishing Group
Birch Lane Press is a registered trademark of
Carol Communications, Inc.
Editorial Offices:
600 Madison Avenue, New York, N.Y. 10022
Sales and Distribution Offices:
120 Enterprise Avenue, Secaucus, N.J. 07094
In Canada:Canadian Manda Group,
P.O. Box 920, Station U, Toronto, Ontario M8Z 5P9
Queries regarding rights and permissions should be addressed to
Carol Publishing Group,
600 Madison Avenue, New York, N.Y. 10022

Carol Publishing Group books are available at special discounts for
bulk purchases, for sales promotion, fund-raising, or educational pur-
poses. Special editions can be created to specifications. For details,
contact: Special Sales Department, Carol Publishing Group,
120 Enterprise Avenue, Secaucus, N.J. 07094

Manufactured in the United States of America
10 9 8 7 6 5 4 3 2 1
Design by Stark Design

Library of Congress Cataloging-in-Publication Data
Bean, Orson.
25 ways to cook a mouse / for the gourmet cat / by Orson Bean. p.cm.
"A Birch Lane Press book."
 ISBN 1-55972-199-5
1. Cookery—Humor. 2. Cats—Humor. 3. Mice—Humor.
I. Title. II. Title: Twenty-five ways to cook a mouse.
PN6231.C624B43     1993
641.5'0207—dc20     93-24145 CIP

For

Michele,

Max, Susannah,

& Zeke From

a Proud Father

# WHY A COOKBOOK FOR CATS?

**C**ats are not dogs. Dogs will eat anything. Cats are noble. They were worshiped in Egypt, and they know it. Cats are our equals and may be smarter than we are. We get dogs to work for us. Cats get us to work for *them*.

In these pages, you will fathom the mysteries of feline cuisine. You will find out what Don Vito Corleone's cat liked for dinner. You will learn the secret recipe that famed New Orleans chef Jean-Claude Melman prepares for his pet. You will read how the preferred dish of Mahatma Gandhi's cat has become a favorite of today's trend-setting cats. And you will discover how Adolf Hitler's cook quietly created a culinary masterpiece for the late-unlamented Führer's feline.

Cats deserve their own cuisine. It already exists. This cookbook creates nothing new – it simply collects and catalogs existing recipes. A well-fed cat is a happy cat who spreads joy in a household. A discontented cat spreads gloom.

Cats have powers. Do not fool with them. They know this cuisine exists. Other cats tell them. It is good that you have bought this book. Learn to prepare these recipes. Your cat is waiting. Do not annoy him.

Thank you.

*The Author*

# CONTENTS

# SOUTHERN-FRIED MOUSE

**1** This is the traditional dish of Deep South plantation cats, best enjoyed on a well-manicured lawn or under a wisteria-covered porch. Plantation cats, like their privileged masters, enjoyed a great deal of free time. They lived, played, and ate in a leisurely fashion and did so with a style which has largely vanished from the feline world.

Manners were all-important to these southern gentlecats (at least in the presence of their human co-plantationists). Dining was accomplished with flair, and when Sunday dinner was served in the

manor house, a savory plate of Southern-Fried Mouse was also relished by the family feline.

**RECIPE:**

Clean and quarter the mouse; season and shake in a bag of flour.

In a skillet, fry mouse in a 1/4 inch of melted butter until it is a golden brown. Do not overcook, as this will dry and tough- en the mouse.

Serve at once, gar- nished with chopped catnip.

# Barbecued Mouseribs

**2** This dish originated among antebellum slave-quarter cats of the Deep South. On feast days, when a pit was dug and a fire built, heaps of barbecued meat would smoke through the night. And off to the side, smaller heaps would simmer: delicious Barbecued Mouseribs.

Life for human inhabitants of the slave quarters was, needless to say, a far cry from that of residents of the manor house. And, of course, socializing between the two groups was unheard of. But in the subculture of the feline community, a very different story ensued.

Slave-quarter cats habitually consorted with plan-

tation cats, prancing and singing on moonlit nights on the levee and engaging in mutual hunts and lovemaking. And to this day, the class distinction widespread among northern cats is unknown among cats of the Deep South.

# Old-Fashioned Mouseloaf

## RECIPE:

Preheat oven to 350°.

Mix twice-ground mousemeat with a small amount of cereal filler (cats have acquired a taste for cereal from eating commercial cat food) and a little egg yolk.

Salt and pepper to taste (cat's taste).

**3** This hearty dish, a basic working cat's repast, has been a favorite of North American felines since the middle of the last century. Recipes for mouseloaf vary in different parts of the continent. Louisiana cats like their mouseloaf spicy; Canadian farmers' cats prefer theirs made with milk and an egg for binding.

Mouseloaf is a special favorite of military cats stationed on bases around North America.

Form into a loaf and place in a slightly greased pan.

Bake about 30 minutes, basting occasionally with stock made from boiled leftover mouse.

Allow to cool before serving.

# GARLIC MOUSE

**4** This dish is for the cat with epicurean tastes, though this may seem like a redundancy, as all cats are food snobs at heart. Let a mangy and derelict stray show up at your door and be taken in. Filled with gratitude, he'll gobble up scraps and leftovers, then curl up in front of the fire and purr himself to sleep. Within a month, this same cat will turn up his nose at freshly opened tuna, glare balefully at you, and stalk out of the kitchen.

## RECIPE:

One mouse, quartered.

MARINADE: 1 table-spoon sour cream, 1/4 teaspoon Worcestershire sauce, and 1/4 clove garlic, diced.

Marinate mouse overnight. When ready to cook, discard marinade.

Sauté mouse in butter for 10 minutes or until brown.

# Mouse Pot Pie

**5** Mouse pot pie originated in Olde England. King Henry VIII's cat, a randy tom with more wives than his master, frequently commanded the royal chef to prepare his personal favorite, mouse and kidney pie. Dick Whittington's cat, when off his master's ship and safe and dry ashore, was said to have relished a good mouse pie.

Despite its aristocratic origins, Mouse Pot Pie is a dish for the common cat. Some will leave the vegetables. If the creamy gravy has soaked into the pie crust, most cats will enjoy chewing on it.

# RECIPE:

Bake the bottom of the pie crust in advance. This makes for a crunchier crust, which cats enjoy.

Boil chunks of mousemeat until done. Remove from water. Add a few finely chopped carrots and potatoes to the mousewater. Boil these until tender (al dente, the way cats like).

Remove from water.

Add the mouse-meat, vegetables, and a bit of the mouse-water to a traditional white sauce (butter, milk, flour . . . see a *people* cookbook).

Pour into pie dish and top with pie-crust dough.

Bake in a preheated 350° oven until crust is brown, approximately 20 minutes.

Warning: You may find bits of partially chewed crust on the carpet.

# PICKLED MICE FEET

## RECIPE:

Wash mice feet; wrap and tie in cheesecloth to retain shape.

Cover with water.

Add 1/4 onion, 1/4 clove garlic, 1/2 sliced lemon, 2 whole catnip leaves, 1 peppercorn, and 4 cloves.

Bring mice feet to boil, reduce heat, and simmer for 1 hour.

Drain and allow to cool before serving.

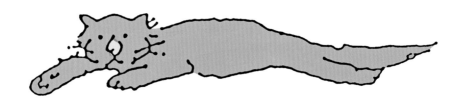

6 This is an offbeat dish for an offbeat cat. Cats of German extraction first introduced Pickled Mice Feet to the felines of North America. It takes a lot of mice feet to fill up a bowl, and they are more chewy than meaty. The recipe is included in this collection so that it will be ethnically correct. Not many cats like Pickled Mice Feet.

"That's not true," says Mrs. Frank Farnsworth's cat, Wilmot. "They are nice to gnaw on in the backyard."

# MOUSE CHOPS AND BANGERS

## RECIPE:

CHOPS: Use only center-cut mouse chops. Broil and season to taste.

BANGERS: Good, commercially produced mousemeat sausages, sweet or spicy, can

**7** This is the national dish of feline Australia: tender, center-cut loin chops of mouse, paired with succulent mousemeat sausages.

Aussie cats in the outback spend their days chasing lizards or being chased by sheepdogs. Then they look forward, with relish, to this superb feline specialty. (Aboriginal cats prefer their mouse au naturel.)

Of course, Australian city cats love the dish, too. A domestic shorthair in Sydney was heard to say, "F'get about shrimp on the barbie, mate. Give me 'MC & B' any day."

be found in better gourmet catfood shops. If you live in an unsophisticated part of the conti-nent and must make your own mouse-meat sausage, follow the instruc-tions in a good *people* cookbook. Substitute mouse-meat for pork or veal and catnip for thyme.

# Mouse Mozzarella

**8** It is said that Don Vito Corleone's house cat, a barrel-bodied manx, loved this dish above all others. Mama Corleone or daughter Connie would always prepare the recipe with great care, as it was not good to annoy the Corleone cat, don of all cats of the five families, *"Il gatto di tutti gatti."*

When the Corleone men "went to the mattresses" (hid out), the manx cat was always there, enjoying food prepared by Clemenza.

## R E C I P E :

Pound slices of
mousebreast into
flattened cutlets.

Dredge through
finely sifted flour,
seasoned with salt
and paprika.

Sauté in a pan with
melted butter.
Do not overcook.

Remove mousecut-
lets and cover with
heated tomato
sauce.

Sprinkle a mixture of
Parmesan cheese and
coarsely chopped
catnip over the top of
each mousecutlet.

Serve warm.

# MOUSE AU POIVRE

**9** This is a classic recipe from France. French cats consider their cuisine to be the finest in the world. English cats, preferring plain boiled mouse and mashed potatoes, scoff at the sauces employed by their continental cousins. But few felines who have tasted Mouse au Poivre can resist it.

This delicious repast should not be introduced to cats with respiratory problems, as the pepper may cause heavy sneezing (though a beneficial by-product of this may be the forced expulsion of fur balls). For a robust cat with a hearty appetite, Mouse au Poivre is a splendid choice.

## RECIPE:

Cut mousesteaks medium thick.

Press the steaks into the crushed peppercorns. In lieu of peppercorns, you may substitute coarsely ground catnip, including stems and twigs.

Sprinkle the bottom of an iron skillet with salt.

Put mousesteaks into skillet and brown, uncovered, on high heat.

Reduce heat, turn mousesteaks, and cook to desired degree of rareness.

# MACARONI AND MOUSE

**10** This is a staple of domestic shorthairs throughout North America. It's a natural combination: cats like mice; mice like cheese; cheese likes macaroni.

Orville Sutter's cat, Daryl, says, "Store-bought mouse and boiled macaroni. That's as gourmet as this old boy needs to get."

## RECIPE:

Boil the macaroni in lightly salted water. Cook al dente.

Cut breast of mousemeat and pound into strips until flat and tender.

In a frying pan, melt a little butter. Do not burn.

Sauté the mouse-meat strips in melted butter until lightly browned.

Drain macaroni. Add mousemeat strips and pour melted butter from frying pan over macaroni.

Add grated cheese.

# CHICKEN-FRIED MOUSE

**11** Chicken-Fried Mouse is one of the great down-home contributions to feline cuisine. White-trash cats have long enjoyed it.

Upscale cats now join them. The idea of a floured crust on a mousesteak appeals to felines who like something crunchy to chew on. The mousemeat need not be the tenderest, as Chicken-Fried Mouse is always well cooked.

Edgar Pinesol's cat, Vern, will eat this dish as often as Edgar will prepare it.

# RECIPE:

Cut mousesteaks medium thick, then flatten with a rolling pin until they are thin and tender.

Sprinkle with salt and pepper.

Flour the mouse-steaks until they are completely white, with no mousemeat showing anywhere.

Fry on both sides in 1/4 inch mixture of hot oil and melted butter. Chicken-Fried Mouse should always be cooked well-done.

Serve with white gravy (see a *people* cookbook).

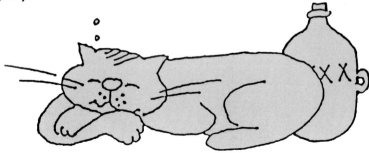

31

# BREADED MOUSE CUTLET

## RECIPE:

Pound slabs of mousemeat until flat and tender.

Dry the mouse cutlets thoroughly, then dredge them in a dish of seasoned flour.

Prepare a mixture of slightly beaten egg, a little water, and a trace of oil. Stir.

Dredge the cutlets through the mixture, then allow any excess liquid to drip off.

Cover mouse cutlets with finely-sifted bread crumbs.

Dry cutlets on a rack for 10 minutes.

Sauté in melted butter on medium heat for 2 minutes.

**12** This is your basic kitten food and a good cheer-up meal whenever your cat feels depressed. Felines, even more than humans, choose their food according to the humor they are in. In a wild and savage mood, a cat may revert to nature and opt for mouse tartar. But, feeling pensive or content, she may choose something mild and civilized, such as Breaded Mouse Cutlet.

This is the true glory of mouse. It can be the basis for any sort of dish and the way to the heart of any cat.

# CREAMED CHIPPED MOUSE ON TOAST

**13** For a damp and chilly afternoon, after hours spent lying in front of the fire, older, semiretired cats find Creamed Chipped Mouse on Toast irresistible.

Many felines regard the toast as a garnish. Others, especially if the crusts are cut off, enjoy it.

## RECIPE:

Open a jar of chipped mouse (available in better gourmet-cat-food shops).

Melt 1 tablespoon of butter. Sprinkle with a tablespoon of sifted flour; stir in slowly.

Add 1/4 cup milk.

Stir.

Pull the chipped mouse apart and add to the sauce. Do not salt.

Simmer ingredients until they thicken.

Remove from heat and season with chopped parsley or chives. (Cats like both. They are good for preventing fur-ball buildup).

Serve on hot buttered toast with crusts cut off. Dust with paprika. (Cats care how things look. They are fastidious in all things.)

# SPAGHETTI AND MOUSEBALLS

**14** This dish has been a staple of Italian cats for generations. While sophisticated northern *"gatti Milanesi"* (cats of Milan) prefer such lighter dishes as *topo picata*, southern felines of Naples and Sicily relish the traditional Spaghetti and Mouseballs.

Vatican cats prefer it to any other dish. One, an aging tom named Fredo, who slept at the bottom of the beds of and outlived three popes, said, "Only *scungilli* do I love more."

## ℞ECIPE:

**SPAGHETTI: Cook the pasta al dente. Drain. (Many cats prefer pasta shells or the chewier rotelle twists.)**

**MOUSEBALLS: Blend a small amount of well-beaten egg (1 egg per 10 mice) to twice-ground mousemeat (lean) and finely chopped catnip.**

**Add salt, paprika, and Worcestershire sauce to taste (cat's taste).**

**Mix in a small amount of seasoned bread crumbs.**

**Form into 1/2-inch balls.**

**Brown mouseballs in frying pan with a tablespoon of butter. Simmer, watching closely until done.**

# Mousetail Soup

**15** A dish for only the most jaded of feline palates. No domestic shorthair will consider it. Winners and runners-up in the angora longhair division of the National Cat Show may relish this exquisite treat. Mousetail Soup is said to have originated in Hungary, where the felines are as charmingly affected as their human counterparts. A joke is told among the cats of Budapest:

CAT: *Waiter, I can't eat this mousetail soup. The mousetail is still wagging.*

WAITER: *Our mousetails come from contented mice.*

## RECIPE:

Brown a dozen mouse tails in 1/2 tablespoon of butter.

Add to this 2 cups of water, a pinch of salt, and 1 peppercorn.

Simmer uncovered for 1 1/2 hours.

Strain, chill, remove fat, and reheat the mousewater.

Bone the mousetail, remove and dice mousemeat, save.

Add 1 tablespoon each of chopped parsley or catnip, finely diced carrots and celery, plus 1 whole catnip leaf.

Simmer 10 minutes.

Brown in pan 1/2 teaspoon of butter and 1/2 teaspoon of flour.

Pour mousestock in slowly and add the saved, diced mouse-tail meat.

Season to taste. On second thought, this sounds so delicious that perhaps any feline will find it irresistible.

Worth a try on the common tabby.

# MOUSE BOURGUIGNON

**16** I got this recipe from a Parisian cat named Maurice. He is unfriendly to American cats as well as to non-Parisian French cats.

## RECIPE:

Marinate 1/4 pound of stewing mouse overnight in red wine (Katz Bros. Kosher).

The next day, remove mousemeat from marinade and sprinkle with flour.

Place in an oven-proof pan with a pinch of salt, 1 peppercorn, 1/2 catnip leaf, and 1/4 clove garlic.

Add marinade; cover and let simmer in 300° oven for 45 minutes. Uncover for last 5 minutes of simmering.

Sprinkle the Mouse Bourguignon with chopped catnip before serving.

# MOUSE IN BLACK BEAN SAUCE

## RECIPE:

Clean the mouse and cut the meat into strips.

Poach the strips briefly in boiling water, then remove and dry.

Heat some oil in a wok. Stir-fry mouse-meat strips until crispy.

Stir in black bean sauce.

Add some bamboo shoots (cats like the chewy consistency).

Warning: An hour later your cat will be hungry again.

**17** Chinese cooking, one of the great cuisines, if not our greatest, has made very limited inroads in the feline world. This is because in China it is an unfortunate fact that a cat is less likely to become a gastronome than he is an ingredient.

Mouse in Black Bean Sauce is, in truth, a pseudo-oriental dish invented in North America in much the same way chop suey was. While delicious, it does fall in the category of trendy cat cuisine. A true Malayan or Javanese will sneer at it.

# CORNED MOUSE
# AND CABBAGE

**18** Corned Mouse and Cabbage is a celebratory meal of Irish "ginger" cats. Traditionally, when a partially grown kitten in Ireland catches and brings home his first mouse, it is corned, cooked, and served with cabbage (the vegetable of the hunt in Irish folklore). Some Irish cats enjoy the cabbage; not many American ones do, but a tradition is a tradition.

## RECIPE:

Purchase a good-sized, precorned piece of mouse at your local cat food store. Or salt the mouse yourself by following the instructions in a good *people* cookbook. (This involves the use of saltpeter, which may keep a wayward, wandering tom at home.)

Wash the corned mouse under running water to remove surface brine.

Cover with boiling water and simmer until a fork can penetrate to the center.

The last 10 minutes, add small wedges of cabbage to the pot.

Always slice corned mouse very thin, diagonally across the grain.

Serve in large cat bowl.

# TANDOORI MOUSE

**19** The house cat of the late Mohandas Gandhi, a wily old short-hair named Sanjit, enjoyed Tandoori Mouse several times a week throughout his lifetime with the beloved Mahatma. Habitually, Gandhi tried to convince his pet of the spiritual superiority of a vegetarian diet, but all in vain.

"You know what you can do with your brown rice," Sanjit's eyes seemed to say.

The recipe for tandoori mouse was brought to these shores by a cat of Pakistani extraction in the wave of feline immigration which accompanied the human influx after World War II.

## RECIPE:

Prepare the following marinade: 1 teaspoon each of plain yogurt, lemon juice, minced garlic, crushed ginger, and ground roasted coriander; 1/2 teaspoon each of dry ginger powder and coarse salt. This will be plenty of marinade for a half-dozen Tandoori mice.

Clean the mouse and cut in half. (It is traditional for tandoori mouse to be served in halves.)

Soak mouse halves in the marinade over night in the refrigerator. It is better that a cat not know that Tandoori Mouse is in the fridge. Cats are not patient.

The next evening, preheat oven to 350°.

Before roasting, brown the mouse-meat in a hot pan. Roast until tender. This gives your mouse the reddish-brown color feline gourmets find irresistible in Tandoori Mouse.

# CAJUN BLACKENED MOUSE

## RECIPE:

Clean mouse and cut into strips.

In a bowl, mix 1 teaspoon each of sweet paprika, salt, onion powder, garlic powder, and ground red pepper. Add 1/2 teaspoon each of whole pepper-corns, ground black pepper, and dried catnip leaves.

Dip mousestrips into melted butter, then into the seasoning.

Heat a large cast-iron skillet for several minutes over a high heat until it is beyond the smok-ing stage and you see white ash on the bottom. The skillet can never be too hot for Cajun Blackened Mouse. Fry mouse strips on both sides until black.

**20** Most North American cats are of mixed ancestry. Our continental melting pot has produced the finest felines in the world: strong, handsome, charming, and of impeccable disposition.

But finest of all is the Creole cat of the Louisiana bayou. There you will find a cat of streetwise, pugnacious, Irish "ginger" extraction who also possesses the aristocratic bearing of a regal Nubian. This sleek and talented cat has long enjoyed the delicacy known as Cajun Blackened Mouse.

Mouse, the *other* white meat, mild by nature, adapts readily to the spiciness of Cajun cooking.

# RATWURST IN BEER

**21** A story is told that Adolf Hitler's pet cat befriended the late German dictator's chef, who, bored with steaming veggies for *der Führer*, concocted the first Ratwurst in Beer for his feline pal.

The term "ratwurst" is actually a misnomer, as ratwurst is made today with only the freshest USDA-inspected mousemeat. In prior centuries in Germany, rat meat was used, and gourmet cats of the day appreciated its gamy flavor and stringy consistency. But today's feline palate demands a kinder, gentler ratwurst.

# RECIPE:

Ratwurst can be made at home. In larger cities, a handful of gourmet feline butcher shops will sell you the casings.

Prepare 1 part minced lard and 4 parts twice-chopped mousemeat. Season to taste with salt, white pepper, and finely chopped catnip.

Add a mixture of chopped onions, warm cream, bread crumbs, and whole beaten egg. Consistency to taste (cat's taste).

Fill the casings 3/4 full, tying with white thread at each end.

Put filled casings into a saucepan of boiling beer.

Reduce heat and cook for 15 minutes.

Remove. Brush with melted butter and grill until golden brown.

You may choose to buy packaged commercial ratwurst. It's a lot easier, and your cat will never know the difference.

# JAMBALAYA MOUSE

In a back alley of the French Quarter of New Orleans, gourmet cats gather at the kitchen door of Jean-Claude Melman's famous restaurant. The great chef is said to own a feline whose proportions are as prodigious as his own. For this lucky cat and his friends, he prepares, on rare occasions, his little-known specialty Jambalaya Mouse, or *"souris chaude,"* as the French Quarter felines call it.

To date, the master has not revealed the recipe for Jambalaya Mouse in any of his great cookbooks.

## R E C I P E :

Prepare a seasoning mix of 1/4 teaspoon of each of the following: salt, white pepper, dry mustard, cayenne pepper, gumbo file powder, garlic powder, and black pepper. Add 2 small whole catnip leaves. Save in a small bowl.

Clean mouse and cut in pieces.

Brown mouse in a frying pan with melted butter or margarine over fairly high heat. Remove and save.

In same pan, brown 1/4 cup each of the following vegetables: chopped onions, chopped celery, chopped green peppers. Stir in 1/2 cup of uncooked rice.

Cook about 5 minutes, stirring constantly and scraping bottom of pan. Add seasonings and 2 cups of mousestock (canned, or make your own by boiling a mouse carcass). Cover and simmer until the rice is tender. Toss in the mousemeat and cook 3-5 minutes more.

Remove the catnip leaves and serve.

# BOILED BRISKET OF MOUSE

**23** This is a dish enjoyed on religious holidays by rabbinical cats and their acquaintances. A saucer of specially sweetened wine may be served on the side.

Kosher mouse may not be easy to obtain unless you live in or near a large city. And remember to apply the rule of separate cat bowls for meat and dairy.

## RECIPE:

Tie the mouse brisket into a compact shape.

In a kettle, melt 1 tablespoon of vegetable oil. Add 2 tablespoons of chopped onions and brown slightly.

Add the brisket and 1 cup of boiling water or mouse-stock.

Simmer for an hour, or until tender.

Season with salt, pepper, and chopped catnip (optional for extremely orthodox cats).

# BURRITOS CON RATÓN

## RECIPE:

Buy premade tortillas or buy tortilla dough and fashion your own tortillas, following the instructions on the package.

Clean and quarter a mouse.

Poach the mouse quarters briefly in boiling water.

Shred the mouse-meat and fry it in a pan with a tablespoon of hot oil.

In the center of a tortilla, place a small portion of chopped lettuce. Add the crispy, shredded mouse, a dollop of sour cream, and crumbled *queso fresco* (the Mexican cheese cats love). Fold over the ends and roll into a burrito.

For the convenience of your cat, cut the burritos into bite-size morsels (cat bite-size).

**24** In the barrios of East L.A. and Spanish Harlem, the pungent aroma of Burritos con Ratón fills the air on a summer night. Chicano cats are street felines, *gatos de las calles.* Moving in packs (gangs), protective of their turf, sometimes violent when a *rojo* cat strays into *azul* territory, these feisty felines are instantly tamed when the scent of Burritos con Ratón wafts into their nostrils.

# Roast Leg of Spring Mouse

*(Souris Printemps)*

## Recipe:

Buy an entire mouse leg (butt and shank). Don't be afraid to select a large one, as mousemeat is almost invariably tender. A good butcher in a feline gourmet shop will help you with this. You may also choose to have the butcher butterfly your leg of mouse.

Preheat the oven to 450°.

Rub the mouse leg with cut garlic and catnip. Place the mouse leg fat side up (if there is any fat—mousemeat is usually quite lean) on a rack in an un-covered, greased pan.

Place in an oven and immediately reduce heat to 325°. Remember to insert a mousemeat ther-mometer (available in better feline gourmet shops).

Roast until internal temperature reaches 175° for well-done, although most European cats like

Parfum des Chats

**their leg of mouse slightly rare (160° to 165°).**

**Serve with traditional catnip sauce. (Follow a mint-sauce recipe in a *people* cookbook, but substitute catnip for mint.)**

**25** This is a classic dish for a Sunday dinner in France. *Chats Français* regard Roast Leg of Spring Mouse as de rigueur for a well-managed ménage. If a cat owner in Marseilles is unable to provide this dish, he will likely find that his *chat* has hit *la rue* in search of a more amenable master.

Cats, in general, feel superior to other species (humans included), and French cats feel superior to all other cats. But all felines relish a *gigot de souris*.

## TWO SPECIAL GOURMET CAT SNACKS:
# MOUSE JERKY

**T**his is a high-protein treat that cats love to chew on.  It's a sign of the culinary times that on weekend evenings, pretty little teenage "mall cats" will be found outside the local shopping center, flirting with the toms and munching on Mouse Jerky. Hardly a gourmet recipe, it is nonetheless included in this book because it is a prime example of nourishing feline junk food.

## RECIPE:

Slice mousemeat into thin diagonal strips. Trim away any fat or membrane.

Salt and pepper lightly or marinate in flat beer and peanut oil seasoned with a little sugar, clove, and finely ground catnip.

Hang the mouse strips from the bars of an oven rack with the oven turned to "warm" (175°). Leave the oven door open to allow moisture to escape. The jerky should be ready in 2-3 hours.

You may want to put your cat out, as he will otherwise be waiting underfoot the entire time.

# SWEDISH MOUSEBALLS

**T**his is not as cruel a dish as it sounds, or as wasteful. Formed from minced mouse-meat, cereal filler, and a sprinkling of ground catnip, the mouseballs are traditionally served as a backyard snack on nights when the moon is full and friends have come to call.

## R E C I P E :

To twice-ground, lean mousemeat, add well-beaten whole egg (1 egg per 10 mice) and finely chopped cat-nip. Season with salt, paprika, and Worcestershire sauce to taste (cat's taste).

Add a small amount of seasoned bread crumbs and form into 1/2-inch balls.

Brown the mouse-balls in a frying pan with a tablespoon of butter.

Simmer on low heat until done. Yum.